GEOGROPHY.   331

WORKING LIFE

OLIVIA BENNETT.

CAT. NO. 246.

GEOGROPHY.

&

GEOLOGY. X

Working Life

Olivia Bennett

Macmillan Education
in association with the
Save the Children Fund and
the Commonwealth Institute

WORKING·LIFE
Acknowledgements

The author and publishers wish to acknowledge the following photograph sources:

Angela Bainbridge   34(R), 35(B), 36(T), 37(L&R)
Christian Aid   6(R), 22(B/L), 22(B/L)
Compix   2/3, 7(T&B), 8(T&B), 9(L&R), 10(B/L), 11, 13(T/L), 13(C/L), 20(B), 21(B), 25, 27(B), 31(T), 32(T), 33(T), 34(L), 35(T), 36(B), 44(L), 45(T&B), 46(B), 47(T).
Peter Davis   16(T), 17(L), 24(T&B), 25(inset), 30(R), 39(T&B), 40(T&B), 41(T&B)
Richard & Sally Greenhill   4(T&B), 5(T&B), 6(L), 10(T), 10(B/R), 12(T/R), 14(L)(T/R), 17(R), 18(T&B/R), 19(T/L), 23(R), 30(L), 31(T), 32(B), 43(R), 46(T), 47(B)
Sarah Hobson   12(L)
R. R. Hodson   19(T/R)&B), 27(T)
Alan Hutchison Library   1, 13(R), 14(B/R), 15(T&B), 2(B/R) & (T/R), 26(T&B), 33(B)
Overseas Development Administration   20, 21, 21(T/R), 38(T)
C. Sanders   42(T&B)
D. Sander   44(T/R)
The Save the Children Fund   16(B), 38(B)
R. Tames   43(L)
The publishers have made every effort to trace the copyright holders, but where they have failed to do so they will be pleased to make the necessary arrangements at the first opportunity.

© 1982 Save the Children Fund and Macmillan Education Ltd

First published 1982

Published by
Macmillan Education Ltd
London and Basingstoke
Associated companies and representatives throughout the world

ISBN 0 333 31196   5

Series design: Mushroom Production · London
Layout: Mel Saunders
Artwork : Anne Julia Dawson
Printed in Hong Kong

This series of books has been produced in collaboration with the Save the Children Fund, and the Commonwealth Institute, to whom the publishers are grateful for their co-operation in finalising the text and selecting the illustrations.

Contents

Acknowledgements   2

Working life   4

Working in subsistence and cash economies –
   Sri Lanka   7

Why do people do the work they do?   10

Division of labour   14

Changes in working life – Kenya   20

Labour intensive work   22

Workers on the move   23

Children working   26

   Shariar the weaver – Iran   28

The rhythm of working life   30

Working the land – two lifestyles in Malaysia   34

The links between working worlds   37

   The market-place   38

A small business – Morocco   39

How is the business run?   42

The holiday business   44

Time off from work   46

Index   48

Working life

Working life. Making a living. What do these phrases make you think of? Wage packets or salary cheques? Rush hour traffic or bus queues? Factories and offices? Is work something that is done outside the home and only at certain times of the day and week? Or is it something that goes on all around you? If you lived on a farm or above the family shop it would go on all around you. How much do you know about your parents' jobs? Have you ever seen where they work or what they do each day?

Do your parents use their working skills at home too? If your dad is a painter he may have decorated your home. If your mum is a teacher you will probably know what she does each day. Perhaps she even helps you with your school work. If she works in an office you might find it more difficult to imagine her working day. How much does your school tell you about the working lives of different people? What does it teach you about the sort of working life you might expect to have? Make a list of all the jobs which you know something about.

How much do you know about your parents' jobs? Do you know what they do all day? Have you been to the place where they work?

What sort of picture comes into your mind when you think about work? Is it a scene like this, or a busy office, a crowded classroom, or outdoor work on a farm?

Perhaps your mother does not go out to work. You may think that you know what her working day is like because she is at home. But can you list everything she has to do? Many housewives feel that they are doing a job of skill just as much as anyone in a factory or office. After all, running a home is just like running any small business and it involves a very wide range of skills. To keep a family home running smoothly you need to be a cook, a book-keeper, a nurse, a cleaner, a decorator, a seamstress, a manager and probably a bit of a plumber and electrician as well. That's quite a lot of talents, isn't it?

Many years ago, running your home would have involved even more skills. Families had to be much more self-sufficient. This means that they had to supply most of their needs, such as food, shelter and clothing, themselves. There were no fridges so food had to be salted, smoked, dried or pickled to preserve it through the winter. There were no washing machines so the weekly wash could take all day. What other tasks can you think of that would have taken longer than they do now? Just keeping the family fed and sheltered was almost a full-time job. The family home was really a centre of working life as well as family life.

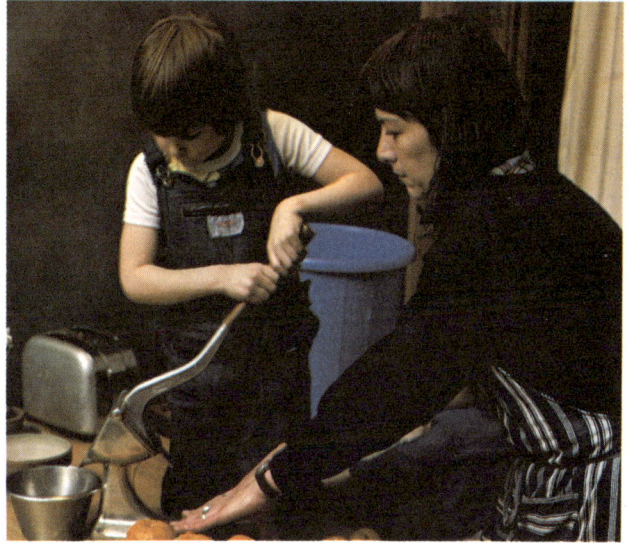

Keeping a home running smoothly is a skilful job. You need to be able to do all sorts of things from cooking food to mending fuses and nursing children with chickenpox. Many people run their homes today with the help of fridges, freezers, cookers, washing machines and other appliances.

Today, if you live in one of the world's more industrial countries, it is likely that your parents have specialised jobs in an office or factory outside your home. For this work they are paid money. With the money they buy goods, such as food and clothes, and services, such as plumbing, which other people are specialising in doing, making or selling. So we are not really self-sufficient any more. We pay other people to build and heat our homes, grow our food, and make most of our belongings, even our entertainment.

Specialisation is an efficient way of working. A man who concentrates on making shoes all day can make them more efficiently than a man who is doing other things as well. It is worthwhile for the shoemaker to make special tools so that he can work quicker, then he can produce enough shoes to sell to others. He moves from working in a **subsistence economy** (in which he produces just enough to satisfy his needs but not enough to buy or sell anything) to a **cash economy** (in which he produces goods to sell for cash). Let's look more closely at the difference between these two ways of working.

People in industrial countries are not as self-sufficient as they used to be. Their work is more specialised. Only builders build houses. Families do not make their own shelters.

Specialisation can be a more efficient way of working. A man making shoes all day can make them more quickly than a man who does other things as well.

Working in subsistence and cash economies - Sri Lanka

Although the self-sufficiency we describe on page 5 is not very common in industrial countries today, it is still the way of life for millions of people, particularly in African, Asian and South American countries. Here most of the people still live in the countryside and make their living from the land. Families and communities in these areas still make most of the things they need by using the natural resources around them. Let's have a look at a family who live in this way in Sri Lanka.

Amil lives with his family in a three-roomed house which they built from the sturdy trunks and huge leaves of the coconut palm. The house is hidden by tall fruit trees and palm trees but you can tell where it is by the 'clak clak' noise of Amil's mother's wooden loom. She weaves most of the family's clothes. Amil's father owns a little land, on which he grows just enough rice to feed the family throughout the year. They also have a small garden in which they grow vegetables and herbs and spices. They use the herbs and spices to make curry which they eat with rice every day.

Amil's family built and thatched their house with materials from the coconut palm. The coconut and its hairy shell also provides them with food, drink, fuel, cooking oil, bowls, spoons, ropes and mats.

Amil lives in Sri Lanka. His family do not have any of the modern machines that you saw on page 5. They make most of the things they need from the natural resources around them.

7

Amil's father is a subsistence farmer. He has some land on which he can grow just enough rice to feed the family. He does not have any left over to sell.
Amil's mother sifts the rice grains with a basket woven from palm leaves. The mat was made in the same way.

Farming families like Amil's, which can only grow enough food to feed themselves, are said to be living at subsistence level. By hard work on their land they have enough to eat, but there is never any extra left over. Therefore they have nothing to sell to make money to buy things which they cannot grow or make themselves.

Some of the other villagers have more land. They can grow more than enough rice to feed their families and sell the extra, or they can grow **cash crops** (crops which are grown to make money) like rubber. Their hard work provides them not only with food but also with cash. With this cash they can build a house out of bricks, buy clothes, radios, bicycles and other belongings and eat fish and meat more often. They can also buy better farm tools, seeds and fertiliser to increase their harvests. This way, they can make more money and perhaps even buy more land. It is very hard for a subsistence farmer to do any of these things.

8

Even in a village where most of the people farm for a living there is a need for a few people with specialised occupations, such as potters, basketmakers, carpenters and blacksmiths. These people produce and repair the goods and tools which farming families need. In Amil's village there is also a small shop selling salt, bread, fruit, dried fish, oil lamps and kerosene oil. A piece of old rope is always smouldering gently by the counter so that passing villagers can light their cigarettes.

In the past, a farmer might exchange some food he had grown for a new storage pot or a mended plough. This system of **barter** or exchange is one step between subsistence and cash economies. Today money, rather than goods, is exchanged. When Amil's father needs a farm tool repaired, he needs money to pay the blacksmith. When Amil's mother goes to the shop for some salt, she needs money to buy it. Because Amil's father does not have enough land to grow cash crops, he works whenever he can for some of the richer farmers in the village. This is the only way he can move beyond subsistence level. It is hard work because he has his own rice crop to look after too, so everyone in Amil's family, including his grandparents, lend a hand.

In order to make some money, Amil's father (right) works for some of the villagers who have more land. Here he is helping prepare the land for sowing.

Everyone in the family has to help on the land. This is Amil's grandfather, praying for a good harvest. Around his waist he is wearing a sarong woven by Amil's mother.

9

Why do people do the work they do?

Some of the traditional crafts of Amil's village have changed over the years. Most of the villagers now buy china bowls and pots which last much longer than the locally-made ones. The village no longer has its own potter. The blacksmith is still busy though. He is over seventy years old and his son and grandson work with him now. His family have been the village blacksmiths for as long as anyone can remember.

If you live near a village, find out if there are any craftsmen left, and which crafts used to be practised. Why have the old crafts died out? You may discover that some of the crafts were always practised by different generations of the same family. Quite often trades and skills are handed down from parents to children for years, like blacksmithing in Amil's village. Is there a traditional working life that has been followed by members of your family for many years? Are any of your older brothers or sisters going into the same trade as your parents or grandparents?

Are any traditional crafts practised in your area? Have any of them been practised by the same family for generations? Have generations of your family always done the same work?

This man has taken up the work for which his village of Oberammergau in West Germany is famous. He carves and gilds wooden religious statues.

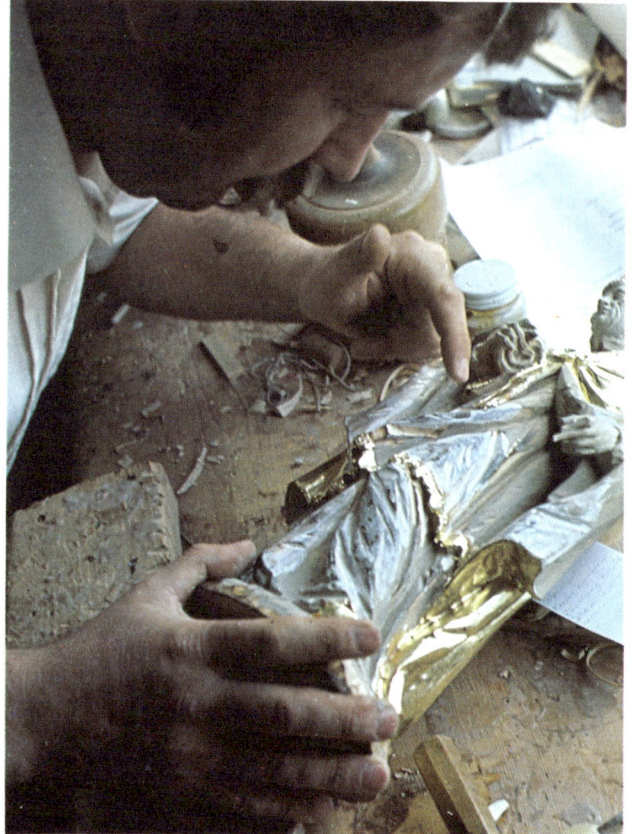

The blacksmith in Amil's village is over seventy years old.

These Tamil women are picking tea in the hill country of Sri Lanka. They are doing exactly the same work as their ancestors were brought over from India to do.

What other things could influence the kind of work you grow up to do? There are traditions outside the family which might affect your choice of work. You might take up the traditional craft of your town or village, like the man in the picture. He is gilding one of the religious statues for which his West German village of Oberammergau is famous. Is there a town or village near you which specialises in a certain type of work? Why do you think that particular craft developed?

In some parts of the world tribal traditions may influence your choice of work. For example, the Ibibio of Nigeria are famous for their wood carvings and masks, while the Luo of Kenya are traditionally fishermen and tailors.

There can be a historical reason for the work that people do, as with the Tamil tea-pickers of Sri Lanka. When British planters introduced tea to the island in the nineteenth century, they brought many Tamils over from their home state of Tamil Nadu in India to work on Sri Lanka's new tea estates. The Tamils lived and worked on the estates and their children grew up knowing no other way of life. They too became tea-pickers. Their descendants are still doing the same work, generations after the first Tamils came to Sri Lanka.

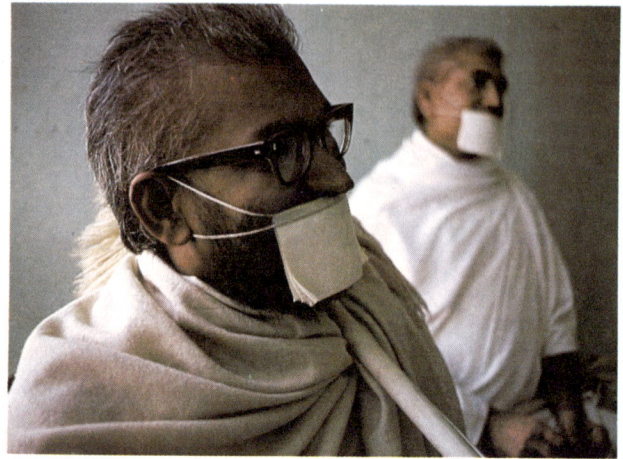

Jains believe that violence against any living thing is wrong. This man's mask prevents him from breathing in tiny insects and accidently killing them.

A Brahmin priest in South India. The Brahmins are at the top of the caste system. They are usually scholars or act as priests for all the higher castes.

If you lived in India, the caste your family belonged to might influence the kind of work you did. Indian society is divided up into five main **castes**. Every Hindu is born into the caste of his father. This often means he is born into a certain type of work too. Strict Hindus only eat with, and marry into, families of the same caste. Many kinds of job (priest, scholar, farmer, blacksmith, potter, goldsmith, tailor or shopkeeper) are only done by members of a particular caste, who live and work together.

The houses in many Indian villages today are still grouped according to caste. But now more people travel, work together in factories and offices, and eat together in restaurants, so the restrictions between castes are beginning to break down, especially in towns and cities.

Sometimes religion affects the choice of work you do in a slightly different way. The Jains, another Indian religious group, believe that violence against any living thing is wrong. Because of this belief, they cannot use a plough to turn over the soil in a field because small worms and insects would be killed or hurt by the action of the plough. Farming is therefore an impossible way of life for them and many take up business or banking as a working life. This kind of job fits in better with their religious beliefs.

The area in which you live can also mean that your choice of work is limited. Some countries rely very heavily on growing and selling one particular crop. For example, in The Gambia it is groundnuts (peanuts) and in Mauritius it is sugar. This means that many of the working people in these countries find work in the cultivation, processing and selling of these particular crops.

Cutting sugar cane in Mauritius. It is the country's main crop and almost everyone on the island works with sugar in some way.

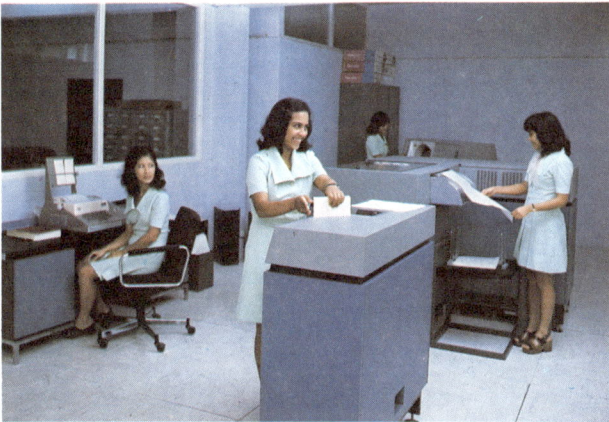

Even most of the office jobs in the country are to do with the sugar trade. These Mauritian girls are operating sugar grading computers.

For example, if you lived in Mauritius you would probably be working on a sugar plantation. Even if you had an office job it would almost certainly be in the sugar trade. Even if you owned a small grocery or hardware store your business would still depend on the sugar crop. A bad harvest would mean low wages for the workers who would then have less money to spend on the goods in your shop.

Countries like Mauritius are trying hard to develop new industries and grow different crops so that the whole country's working life and economy are not dependent on one product. The same sort of thing can happen in an area where a community has developed around one particular industry such as coal-mining, steel production or oil-drilling.

Almost everyone in this Welsh village works in the coal mine, for the same reason that so many Mauritians work in the sugar trade. It is because there is no other work in the area.

Division of labour

We have looked at why some people take up certain trades, skills and professions. Now we are going to look at how people divide the work between each other. The sharing out of jobs between people is called the **division of labour**. Think about the division of labour in your own home and between the different members of your family. Are most of the chores shared equally or do you each have a particular job which is your own responsibility? Do you take turns to do the housework, the cooking or the washing up?

Think about your school too. How is the division of labour organised there? Who does the jobs like supervising playtime and keeping order at mealtimes? Do you belong to a club like the Brownies, Cubs or Scouts? Is there a leader of your pack or group? Who decides which members are to do certain jobs or duties?

Does one member of the family always do the cooking or do you take turns? Who does the washing up afterwards?

The sharing out of different types of work between people is called the division of labour. How is the work divided in your own home?

In societies where the people live by hunting and gathering food the division of labour between men and women is usually very clear cut. The men, like these Brazilian Indians, go on hunting trips while the women gather food from the area near their homes.

Another division of labour you might think about is the one between men and women. Today, these divisions are most strict in societies based on agriculture and in societies where the way of life has changed little over the years. An example of a very simple division of labour can be seen among people who survive by hunting and gathering their food. The hunting of animals is done by the men and the gathering of wild fruits, vegetables, plants and small grubs is done by the women.

This division of labour is very practical and it would be difficult to mix these jobs. The men's hunting trips may mean several days, or more, away from home. While the men are away the women can stay at home with the children, making only short trips to gather food from the surrounding countryside. Hunting and gathering people do not usually stay in one area for very long because the supply of food growing around the camp or home would soon run out. Instead families, or whole tribes, move on to new areas at regular intervals so that the old areas can recover and the food supply can grow again.

15

In more settled agricultural communities, where people cultivate the land and grow crops, the work of crop growing (particularly in Africa) is usually done by the women. Looking after animals is often the man's job.

Market trading is another job which is done by the women, in Africa. There are some societies, however, where the market traders and stallholders are always men. Bangladesh is one example. Bangladeshi village women are meant to spend most of their time in the family compound. Only the men go out to the fields, to the mosque, to the market and other meeting places.

Market trading can give women quite a lot of power and independence because it means that they control the flow of money into the family. In traditional fishing communities women almost always take on the job of selling the fresh catch. This leaves the men free to go out to sea and bring in more fish. Trading is particularly important in fishing communities because families cannot live solely on what they catch in the sea. They need to exchange the fish for other foods, such as rice and vegetables, which a farming family can produce for itself from its land.

The division of labour is not the same in every society. In traditional fishing villages, like this one in Kampuchea, women usually take on the job of selling the catch so that the men are free to go out to sea again.
In most African countries market trading is women's work but this market in Upper Volta is run by men.

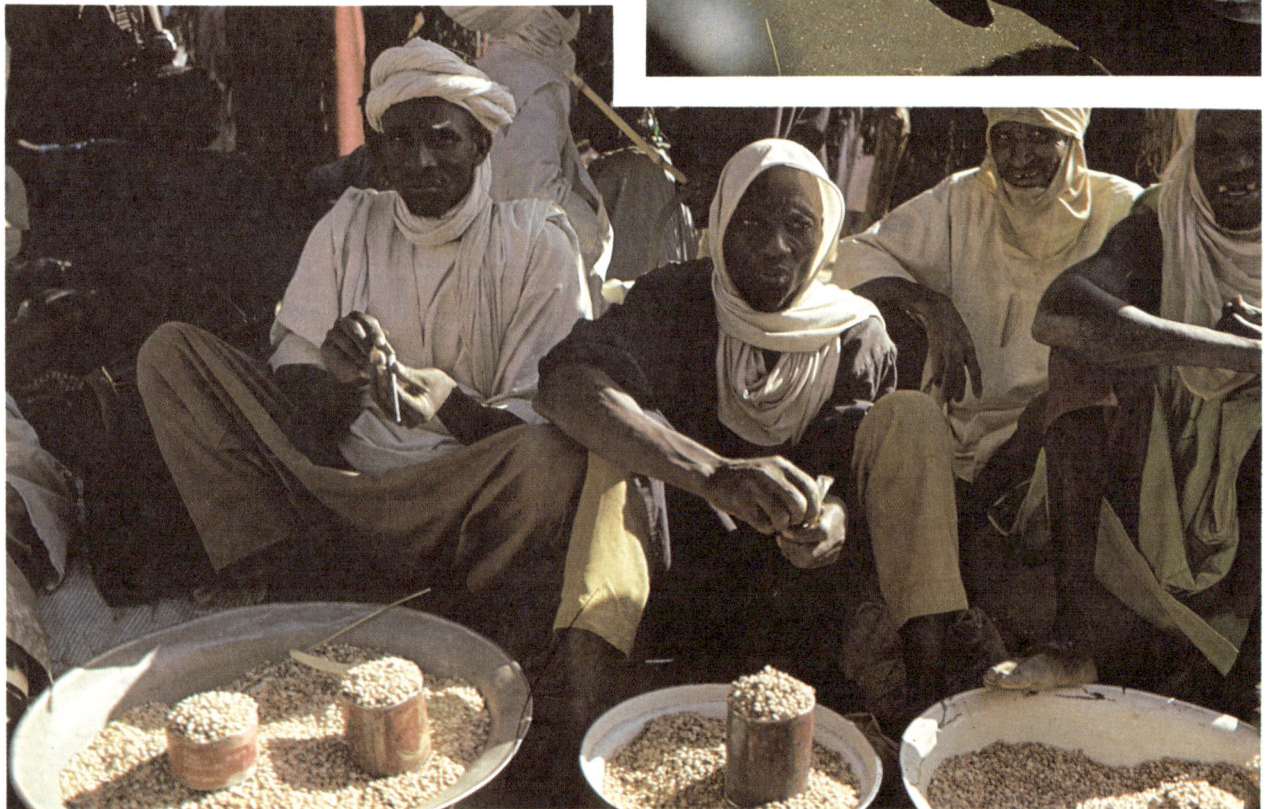

Sometimes the division of labour is more a result of outside events. Pictures on this page show women in Kampuchea working in salt beds and making a fishing net. The women have always made the nets while the men were away in their fishing boats, but they have not always worked in the salt beds. This was traditionally a man's job. Kampuchea is recovering from a long period of great suffering and fighting. Many Kampuchean men died in the fighting. This is why lots of jobs which used to be done by men are now being done by women. Otherwise, they would not be done at all.

Just as trading is done by the men in some countries, and by the women in others, so certain jobs in other societies are treated differently. To the Naga people who live in north-eastern India, making mats and baskets is men's work while the Iban people of Borneo regard it as women's work. The Iban would be most amused to see a man doing such a job. Housebuilding in most societies is done by men but the houses of the Pueblo and Zuni Indians of New Mexico and Arizona were always built by the women.

Making the fishing nets has always been traditional work for Kampuchean women in fishing communities.

Kampuchean women carrying salt. This used to be a man's job but since the war which caused the death of many men, women have taken on much of their work.

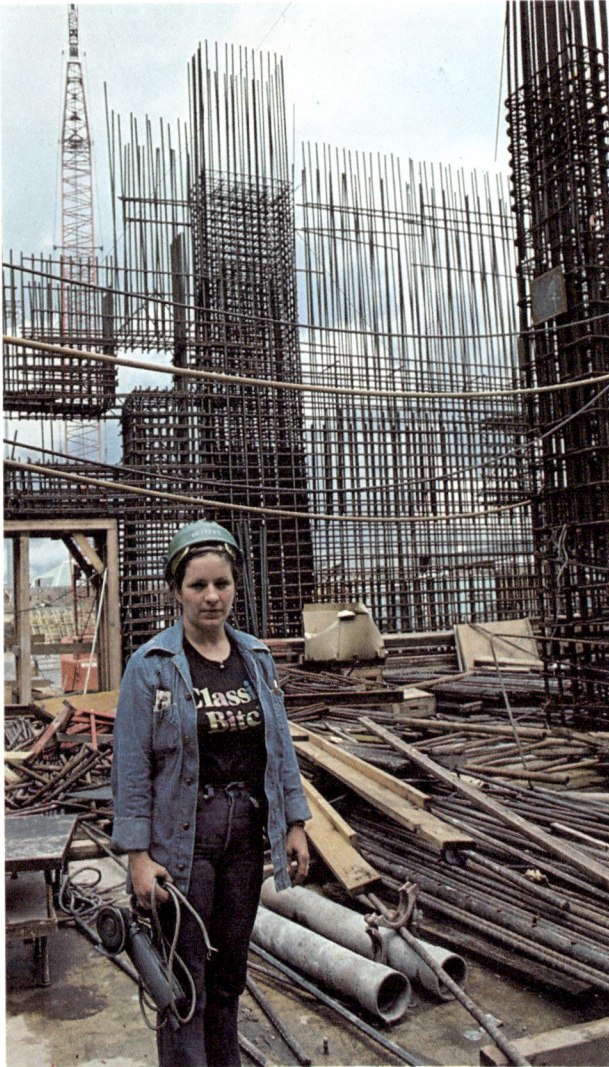
A woman worker on the site of an American power station. Women are beginning to take up jobs which, just a few years ago, were only done by men.

Peoples' ideas about the division of labour are often so strong that they are extremely difficult to change. Something, such as the war in Kampuchea, has to force the change. In Britain, after the outbreak of World War One, women replaced men in all kinds of work. Try and find out what sort of jobs they took over. What happened after the war ended?

The sight of men doing something traditionally regarded as women's work is often the cause of much laughter, and sometimes scorn. On the other hand, women taking on men's work are sometimes treated with resentment and suspicion. To this day some skilled North Sea technicians will not allow women on oil rigs because they fear that they will bring bad luck with them. Can you find out what superstition this comes from?

Many of these **taboos** or restrictions about who does which job still exist, but some people are trying to break down these divisions. They feel that an individual ought to have the choice of any kind of job, not just those which are considered to be suitable for him or her.

In recent years one of the most well-known attempts to change people's ideas and attitudes to the division of labour has been made by the **women's liberation movement**. One of the movement's aims is to break down the traditional divisions of labour between men and women. They want to give women the freedom to choose the kind of work they do, and to open up many more working possibilities for them.

What jobs do your parents do? Can you imagine them doing each other's jobs? If not, why not? Is it because they really do not have the right skills or abilities? Or is it because you have always thought of the job your mother does as women's work, and the work your father does as a job for men? At home who does the cooking and the housework? Are the household chores shared? If you have an older brother and sister, try and think whether there is any difference between the sort of jobs they have or are looking for? Does your sister have more choice about the sort of work she can do than your mother did when she was young?

A woman construction worker in the United States.
A woman police officer in the United States.

A postwoman is still quite an unusual sight in America, but can you think of any reasons why there should only be postmen?

There are many women in the world whose working lives have changed little over the years. Just keeping their families fed, clothed and sheltered is a full-time job.

Changes in working life - Kenya

There are many millions of women in the world today whose working lives are the same as they have been for centuries. They grow the family's food and have no modern kitchen machines to help them prepare it, perhaps not even running water. Yet they often have a lot of power and influence in the family and the community, and a change to a more modern working system does not always improve their situation. We shall look at an example of this now.

The Kenyan family in our picture used to live on a smallholding in the countryside. There were several huts in which different members of the family lived, a garden or **shamba** where the mother grew most of the family's food, and a small cattle pen. The father looked after the animals and took odd jobs whenever he could. They were not well-off but they were nearly self-sufficient.

A Kenyan family in their smallholding. This contains the huts in which they live, a cattle pen and a shamba (garden) where the mother grows most of the family's food.

The family moved near a sugar plantation and now grow sugar cane in their smallholding. The father takes the cane to this mill and exchanges it for cash.

The father of this Kenyan family also gets work cutting cane on the plantation. The family has more money to spend now but there is no room in the smallholding to grow any food.

New schemes, like the sugar plantation scheme, now try to make sure that women can keep their shambas and continue to provide the family's food.

Then the family decided to move near a big sugar plantation some kilometres away from their old home. They still live on a smallholding but it is completely covered with sugar-cane. The father takes the cane to the huge sugar mill and exchanges it for cash. He also gets part-time work on the mill's own plantation.

The family now has much more money to spend than it had before but, because the entire smallholding is taken up with sugar cane, there is no shamba and the mother has to buy all their food instead of growing it. She now depends for food on the few shops that have opened up in the area. She often has to buy more expensive goods (such as tinned or processed food) than the family really wants or needs. In fact the change in working life has altered their whole pattern of family life because the division of labour in the family has changed.

Because the mother no longer has a shamba, she has to ask her husband for money every time they need food. She has lost much of her independence and control over the family's welfare. If the sugar crop fails, or her husband falls sick or leaves home, she and the children will be worse off than before. Today, new schemes make sure that families have enough space to keep their shamba going. Their pattern of living then remains the same and the mother continues to provide the family's main food herself.

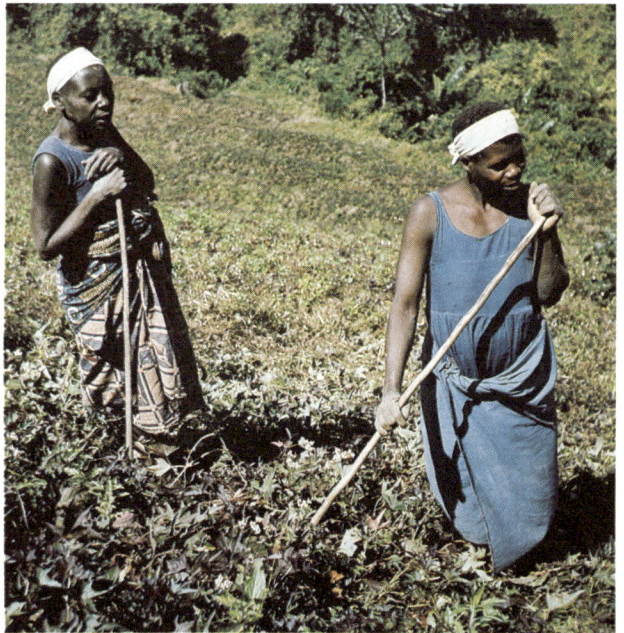

Labour intensive work

One of the biggest changes to people's working lives came with the introduction of machinery. You can probably think of many jobs which are better done by a machine than a person. There are also a number of jobs which people are happy not to do if a machine can, because they are boring or dirty or unpleasant in some way. In areas where labour is scarce and expensive, it makes sense for a factory owner to install machinery.

However, in many parts of the world, such as India, there are more people needing jobs than there are jobs to go round. In this situation it is better to keep people employed in **labour intensive** jobs than to replace all the people with one or two machines.

So if you visit an Indian building site and see a row of people passing small baskets of bricks or cement from one to another along a line, perhaps you will understand why. Such a labour intensive system is probably the best one for the workers. Would it be better to replace all those people with one machine and have them sit around with no work to do and no way to earn a living?

In countries where there are many more people than jobs, labour intensive ways of working (which use people rather than machines) help to solve the problem of unemployment.

Certain kinds of job are done better by machine than by hand. Can you think of some reasons why?

Workers on the move

Today, more and more countries are finding it difficult to give a job to everyone who needs one. In the past there have been times when certain countries have had the opposite problem. Many European countries, for example, did not have enough people to fill all the jobs in the new factories and businesses that sprang up after World War Two. They encouraged people to come from other countries where jobs were scarce. Some of these **migrant workers** found themselves living in poor conditions and unable to save up enough money to bring their families into the country. Others were able to settle in more easily and make new lives for themselves and their relatives. Often people of the same nationality lived together in the same area. They created a home away from home with shops and restaurants serving and selling the food they were used to.

The movement of people from one country to another in search of work is not a new idea. Perhaps your family originally came from abroad, or from another region of your own country. At school you probably have friends whose parents or grandparents moved to your country in order to find a new kind of working life.

Several of the husbands, sons and brothers of these Turkish women have left their poor country villages to work in Germany.

Sometimes people move to another country to find work. A Turkish shop in Berlin, Germany. Foreign workers of the same nationality often live in the same area and set up shops selling the goods they are used to.

An Altiplano village in Bolivia. Some of the Quechua and Aymara Indians who used to farm this difficult area have moved down to the lowland forest to start new working lives.

Starting a new life means hard work and many changes. The Indians made sure that they brought their old songs and music with them to their new homes.

There are some people who are continually on the move, searching for work in different areas. The Quechua and Aymara Indians normally work the dry and difficult farmland of Bolivia's high mountain plains, the **altiplano**, but every year they come down to the cotton plantations to pick the harvest. Then they return home. Hand-picked cotton gets a better price for the plantation owner than machine-picked cotton. The Indian workers are often badly paid and have to put up with poor living conditions because the owners know they need the work too badly to protest.

Some of the Indians have now left the altiplano. They have given up their land, their homes and their friends, and moved hundreds of kilometres away to set up farms in the thick lowland forest which covers two-thirds of Bolivia. The Government helps them with some of the very hard work that is needed to start a new life like this. The forest is cleared, homes built, crops planted, wells dug, schools and clinics set up and a community created. All this must be done in an unfamiliar landscape and climate.

24

For some, the struggle to make a new life in Bolivia's forest is too difficult. These Indians drift on to the cities and towns in search of work. All over the world, the greatest movement of people searching for work is from the countryside to the cities. It is thought that, every day, about 75,000 people in Africa, Asia and South America uproot themselves from their country farms and villages and head for the towns. All too often they get there to find there are no jobs and the only place to live is a crowded shanty town on the city's outskirts.

Nevertheless, these cities do give the migrants a choice of jobs that they would not be able to do in the country. They set up small one-person businesses on pavements, at street corners and even under flyovers. They make and sell snacks and drinks, repair pots, pans and bicycles, guard parked cars or people's shopping, sell cigarettes, matches or newspapers, deliver goods, or convert bicycles into **pedicabs** to ferry people around the city. Even the city's rubbish provides work. Some collect old papers and rags for recycling into newspaper. Others collect scrap pieces of metal and turn them into cigarette tins, knives and plates.

All over the world the greatest movement of people looking for work is from the countryside to the city. This family moved to Delhi and set up a weaving business.

All sorts of small businesses are set up in the city. This man is repairing bicycles in Phnom Penh.

It is not just grown-ups who struggle to make a living on the streets of the overcrowded cities of Asia, Africa and South America. Children like these two boys in Bogota work too.

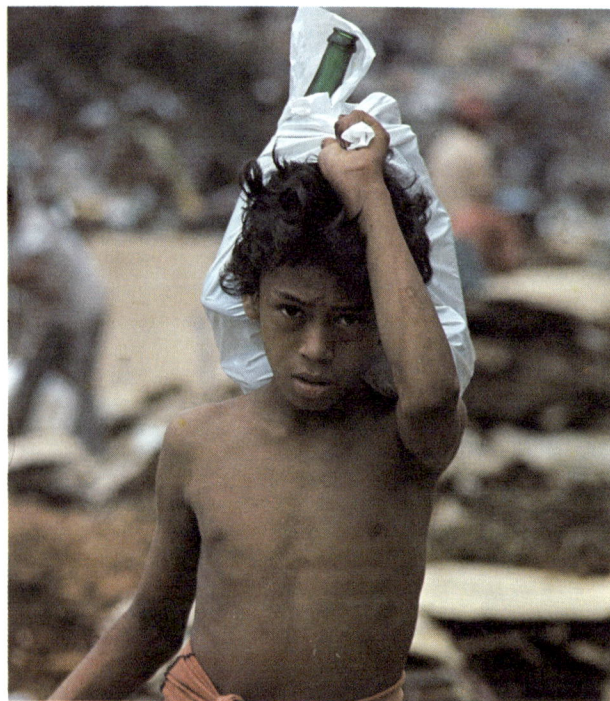

This young boy's job is to collect any rubbish that can be mended, recycled or turned into something useful. Nothing is wasted.

Children working

Grown-ups are not the only ones who struggle to make a living on the streets of the overcrowded cities of Africa, Asia and South America. Young people of your own age, and under, work too. Usually their parents cannot afford to look after them or keep them at school.

Jesus Antonio Pinella is ten years old. He lives and works on the streets of Bogota, Colombia. He says: 'I went to live on the street because my mother is very poor. There are eight children. So I went off to get food for myself. I look after cars for about fifty or sixty pesos a day. Sometimes I stay out all night looking after cars outside the disco. It is difficult living on the street. There is nowhere to wash. I often get cold at night, and sometimes I get sick.'

Luis Tacheco is fourteen years old. He sells cigarettes on the streets of Bogota from eight o'clock in the morning to six o'clock at night, usually without taking a rest. 'I usually sell about twenty packets a day. I get five pesos on each packet. All the money goes to my mother to buy food and clothes. My father tries to get work as a handyman. He only knows how to paint. I earn more than he does.'

In India alone, over sixteen million children work for a living. It is not just in the cities that they start work at an early age. In the countryside, children start to play an important role in the family by the time they are six or seven. At this age they start looking after their young brothers and sisters, while their mothers go out to work in the fields all day. Soon they learn to do all the domestic chores like sweeping and washing. By the time they are ten they become the cowherds and shepherds of the village. They often spend all day on grazing lands with the animals. They also collect fuel and water for the family. By about twelve years old they are working in the fields. They earn half an adult's salary, and at harvest time they can earn even more.

In the Western world, children used to work in very bad conditions in mines, factories and other work places. In England, Parliamentary Bills by people such as Lord Shaftesbury ended child labour in the nineteenth century. Why do you think small children were useful in mines and factories? What sort of jobs did they do?

Many country children also start work at an early age. By the time they are six or seven they have started looking after their young brothers and sisters.

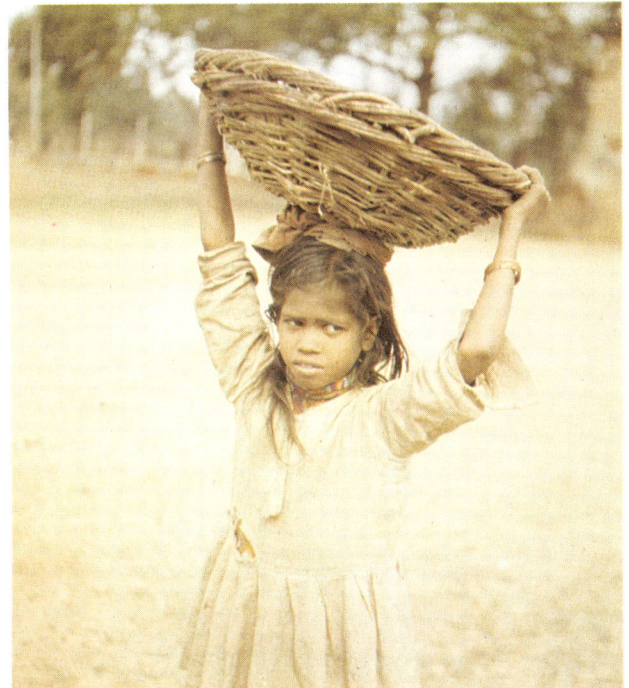

Soon they learn to do all the domestic chores like sweeping, washing and collecting fuel and water. By the time they are ten they are the shepherds and cowherds of the village.

Shariar the weaver – Iran

Apart from working in the home and on the land, young children sometimes take part in more skilled, specialised work. For certain jobs their small, nimble fingers are quicker and neater than those of an adult. Shariar and his family live in a small village in Iran. They are weavers. They make beautifully coloured and patterned carpets. Shariar's eighth birthday was an important day for him. It was the day he began to learn all there is to know about this ancient and skilled craft. From that day on, he became a working member of the family, rather than a child with no responsibilities.

Shariar, with his father, learning to weave a carpet.

28

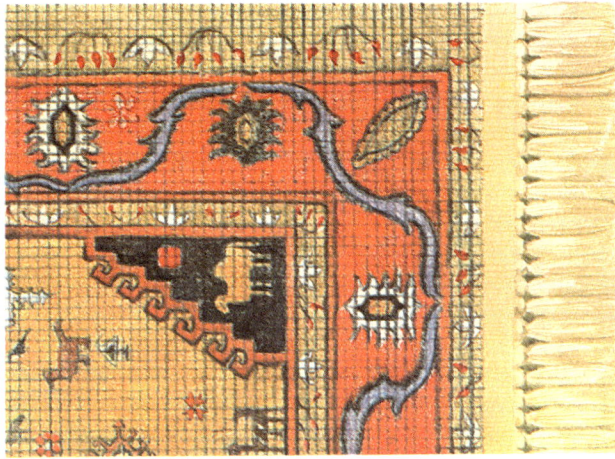

Part of the traditional pattern. What does it show?

'First of all he learnt how to make a loom. This is the wooden frame on which the carpet is woven. Shariar and his father set off by mule to find some poplar trees, which grow particularly tall and straight. The logs used to make the loom must be very straight so that the pattern on the carpet is regular. Then he watched as his mother cut the wool from the family's sheep and washed it, first in the village stream and then in a tub of hot soapy water. After the wool had dried in the hot sun, his mother spun the wool into strands.

Shariar's next lesson was how to recognise and gather the different wild plants whose flowers and roots provide dyes. These give the carpets their rich and glowing colours. After the first strands of wool had been dyed deep reds and blues, Shariar and his father began to design the carpet. They worked out a marvellous pattern. It included pictures of camels, birds, trees and flowers, and they drew it onto the dry mud walls of their small house. Then they could look at the design as they were weaving and as the multi-coloured carpet gradually grew bigger.

Finally, Shariar learnt how to weave the strands of coloured wool backwards and forwards across the loom. It was very hard work but as the weeks wore on and the pattern developed under Shariar's nimble fingers, his confidence and excitement grew. This first carpet took almost a year to complete. By the time Shariar was nine years old he was well on the way to becoming an expert carpet weaver and had settled down to working a long and exhausting day, every day.'

Do you think you could create something so beautiful, yet needing so much patience, at only nine years old?

The finished carpet.

The rhythm of working life

We have already seen that changes in a person's working life can sometimes change his pattern of living. The search for work might lead a family to uproot itself from its familiar surroundings and move elsewhere. A change in ways of working can make a difference to the division of labour and the role of the mother within the family. We saw this in the story of the Kenyan family who started growing a cash crop of sugar cane (see page 20).

Working life can also affect the rhythm of family life, for example the times when everyone is together. And the rhythm of working life is in turn affected by all sorts of things. In a hot country people often start work very early in the morning, before the sun is too high in the sky. They come in the middle of the day for a meal. Then they have a rest or **siesta**, a Spanish word meaning an afternoon nap, and return to work after the sun has lost some of its heat.

In a country like England, the weather is rarely hot enough to make a siesta time necessary. Most people in England get to work around nine o'clock, stay there all day and leave at about five o'clock. Can you find out the school hours in Spain, Australia, Kenya and England? Are they different? Why do you think this is?

Commuters at a London railway station. People's working hours affects the time they spend with their friends and family and their pattern of living.

In hot countries everyone stops work in the middle of the day and shops, offices and streets are almost deserted. This street is in the Moroccan town of Chechaouen.

When do you go on your holidays? Does the time at which you take your family holiday depend on the kind of jobs your parents do?

Some countries work a six-day week, while others work from Monday to Friday. Some jobs are run in **shifts**. Can you think of any jobs like this? Why do you think there have to be shifts? If you did the night shift you would probably find yourself sleeping most of the day, when many other people were out at work. Or you might do an afternoon shift, starting at two o'clock and returning home at about ten o'clock at night. What sort of hours do the members of your family work? How do their hours affect the amount of time you spend together?

Holiday patterns are different all over the world too. In France, most people take their holidays in August and many factories shut down for the month. In England, people can take their holidays at different times but the summer months are usually the most popular. In Sri Lanka, any day on which there is a full moon is a holiday. Do you think you would prefer a system where everyone takes their holiday at the same time? Why do you think it might be easier to run a factory on this system?

Most people like taking their holidays in the summer but if everyone goes away at the same time they sometimes get stuck in terrible traffic jams. Has that ever happened to you?

Farming work has a rhythm of its own. This corresponds more to the changing seasons and the weather than to weekends and official holidays.

A farmer's work follows the pattern of the seasons and so do his holidays and festivals. The harvest festival is one of the most important.

Someone earning his living in an office or factory might find that his working life was quite separate from the rest of his life. His family might never even see his place of work or meet his workmates. Someone working and living on a farm cannot separate work from the rest of his life so easily. Because they live on the farm, they are literally surrounded by their work, and they often work alongside other members of their family. Agricultural work also has a rhythm of its own. This corresponds more to the changing seasons and the weather than to weekends and official holidays.

Any farmer has to do certain jobs at certain times of the year, no matter where he lives. And when the weather is right for a job like ploughing or harvesting, he has to keep working until the job is done. Some months it is more difficult to work on the land. These are quieter times, when the farmer can repair his farm equipment or build a new granary to store the next season's harvest.

Holidays usually tie in with farming events. The harvest festival is one of the most important. It is a time when the whole community can celebrate after the hard work of gathering in the crops.

The pattern of working life in a fishing community depends on the seasons, the weather, the flow of currents and tides, and the movement of shoals of fish.

Families who leave their farms in search of work in towns and cities find that their pattern of living no longer follows the rhythm they are used to. Working hours are more regular, and because jobs are more specialised, the family does not work together as much. It is more difficult to have ceremonies and festivals like the village harvest festival which goes on for several days and involves the whole community.

The pattern of working life in a fishing community is also dominated by the seasons and especially by the weather. Strong winds or storms mean that the fishermen cannot go out and earn their living. Their working lives depend on many things over which they have no control. Some of these are the moods of the sea, the nature of the weather, the flow of currents and tides, and the movements of shoals of fish. This is one reason why fishing communities are often religious communities. They have a strong belief in the spirits or gods which they feel control these factors. Many fishing communities have temples or shrines to the sea. The sea may be good to them and reward their prayers with a large catch, or it may destroy their boats and livelihoods.

The annual Argungu fishing festival in northern Nigeria. All the fishermen compete for the biggest catch and everyone joins in the celebrations afterwards.

Working the land – two lifestyles in Malaysia

To get an idea of the many small ways in which a person's working life can affect his lifestyle, we are going to look at two families in Malaysia. They both live and work in Selangor state and they both make their living from rubber, one of Malaysia's most important natural resources. Rubber is made from **latex**, a creamy white sap which oozes out of rubber trees when a cut is made in the bark. This is called **tapping**. The latex runs into a small cup tied to the trunk. After it has been collected, the latex sets hard. It looks a bit like white blancmange but it is much tougher. It is then processed and made into all sorts of different goods from bicycle tyres to elastic bands.

One of the families works on a smallholding and the other on an estate. Let's see what difference this makes. Alimah Awang is the smallholder. She and her family have a small plot of land on which they grow and tap their rubber trees. The Government lent them the money to buy the land and the rubber saplings. They are gradually paying back the loan and eventually they will own the land themselves.

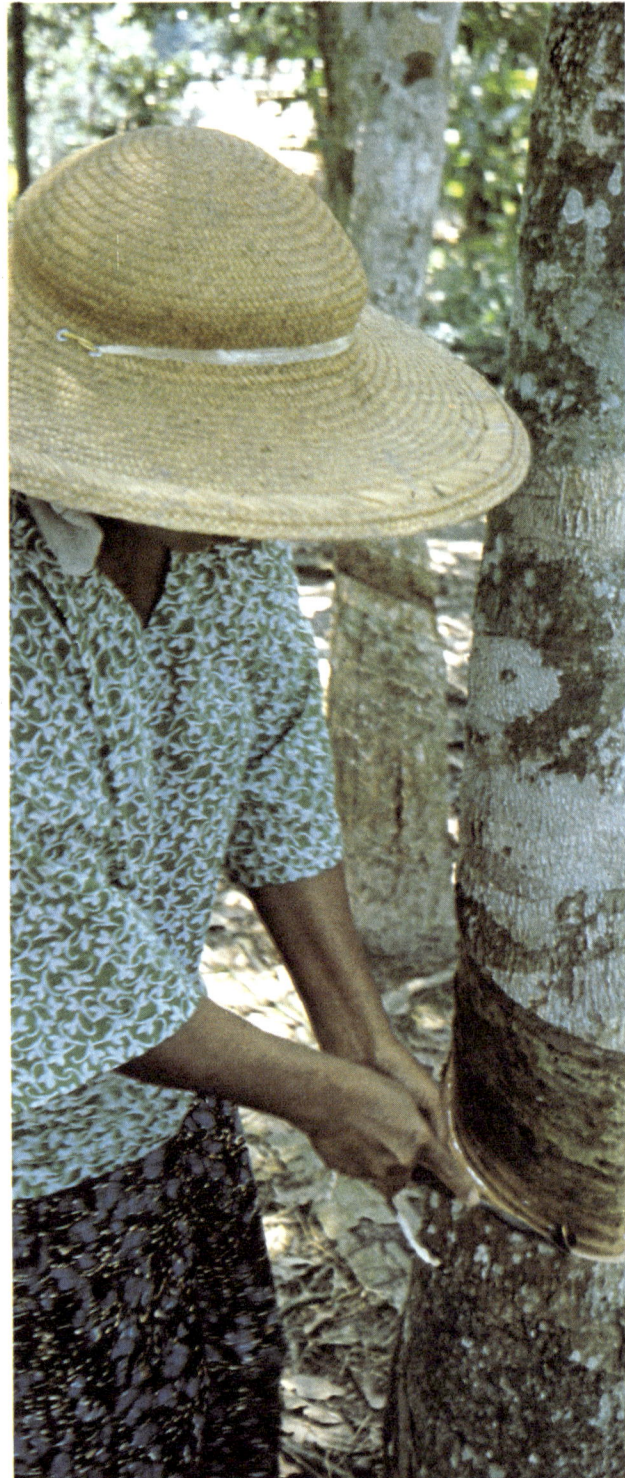

Alimah Awang tapping one of the rubber trees on her smallholding.

Latex dripping from a rubber tree into a cup made from a coconut shell split in half.

Rows of rubber trees on the big estate where Sepak Takraw works. There are so many trees that Sepak is never without work or wages.

Sepak Takraw works on a rubber estate which is owned by a big company. The company employs people to work on the estate. It provides them with housing, a small clinic and primary school, and regular employment. Sepak does not have to worry if the trees get a disease, or if manufacturers want to pay less for the rubber. He does not even have to think about what to do each day. He is usually employed to do one task all the time. It may be weeding, tapping or another job.

Alimah has more responsibility and worries, but her days are more varied because she and her family have to do all the jobs all the time. They see the whole process through from start to finish. She does not earn money every day because the trees should only be tapped every other day. They cannot be tapped when it is raining either, and Malaysia has a long rainy season. Young trees growing up have to be seven years old before they produce good latex. So Alimah relies on other ways of making money too, such as rearing chickens, making **mee** (noodles) or keeping cattle. On an estate there are so many hectares of trees that there are always some ready to be tapped, so Sepak's working life is more secure in some ways.

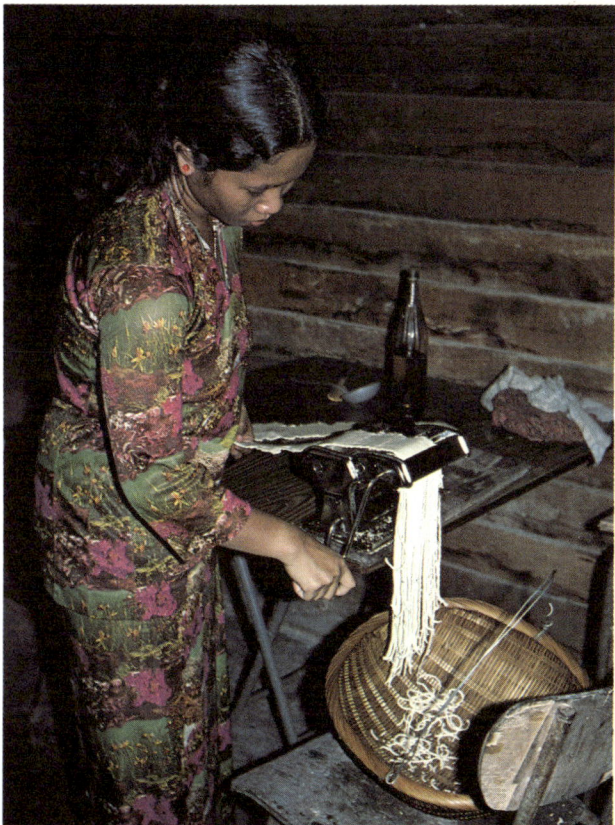

Alimah's smallholding has fewer trees and she cannot rely on earning money from them every day. She makes and sells mee (noodles) like these as well.

Alimah's house in the kampong (village). The houses are built on stilts to protect them from floods and to keep cool air circulating underneath.

Alimah's family live in a **kampong** (village) in a house which they built themselves. The houses are built on stilts to protect them from **monsoon** floods in the rainy season. Each house is surrounded and shaded by tall fruit trees and most of the smallholders also grow food crops in small gardens. Sepak's house was built by his employers. They all look the same. They are set out in neat rows and made of modern materials. When they were built the land was cleared by bulldozers and lots of fruit trees and bushes were destroyed. There is not much room for gardens either.

Some of the smallholders got together and formed a **cooperative.** By working with each other, Alimah and her neighbours could afford to build a well-equipped processing centre. Now they hope to get a better price for their rubber because the processing centre has improved its quality. The centre became quite a meeting place for the villagers, so they built on an extra room for kampong meetings and other activities. Sepak's neighbours do not often work together because their working lives are organised by the estate managers. Perhaps now you can see some of the ways in which the working lives of Sepak and Alimah affect their lifestyles and living patterns.

Alimah's family built their own house but Sepak lives in a house like these. They were built by the estate owners and have strong tin roofs to keep out the monsoon rains.

36

The links between working worlds

Look at the picture below of goods made from Malaysian rubber. How many of them have you used or come across recently? The lives of Alimah and Sepak may seem far away and remote from your own but the working lives of people all over the world are linked in many ways. Just think about your breakfast this morning. Did you have any tea, coffee or sugar? All of these would have been produced by people working in countries thousands of kilometres away. And did you know that nearly half the people working in British manufacturing businesses, for example, make their products with raw materials (like rubber) which come from other countries?

The price that countries like Britain, Japan or Australia pay for Malaysia's rubber has an effect on the country as a whole, and families like Alimah's in particular. If your country's supply of raw materials like rubber, copper, zinc, coffee, tea or cocoa stopped, just think how your family's jobs, diets and way of life would be affected. We are all part of one world and our lives are linked together. Look around your home, your school, the streets and the local shops. How many things can you find that were grown, mined or otherwise produced by people working in other countries?

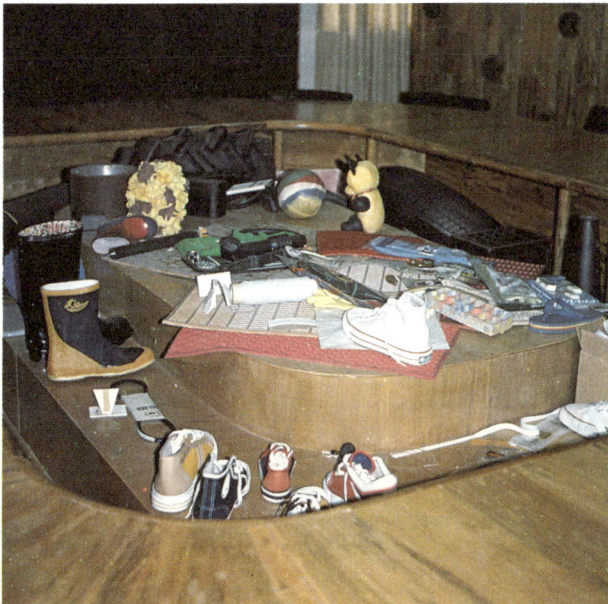

Trays of latex at the kampong processing centre. The centre has improved the quality of the smallholder's rubber. It has also become a meeting place for the villagers.

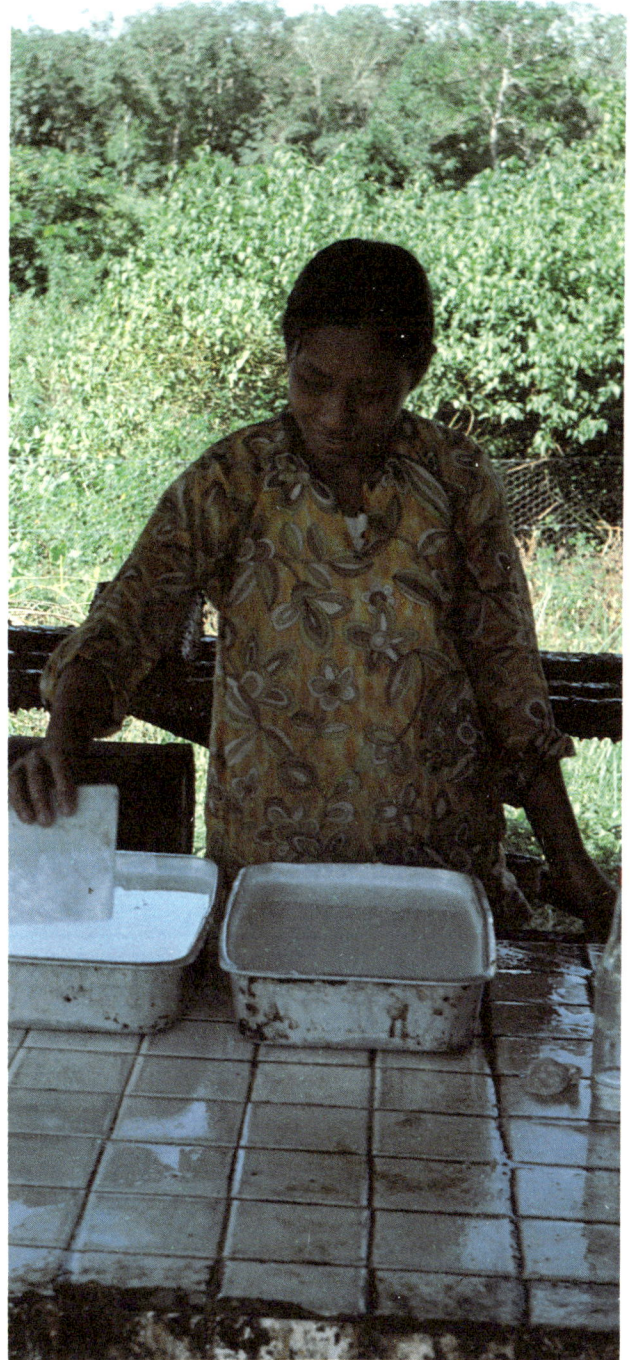

How many of these goods made from Malaysian rubber have you used recently? How often do you eat or use things made from raw materials which come from other countries?

37

The market-place

World trade is rather like a big version of a village market. Countries, rather than people, bargain with one another over prices for products like rubber, copper, coffee and jute. Those countries which only produce one major crop, such as tea or bananas, are in the same position as the man who comes to market with nothing but lemons. If it is the lemon season, lots of other people will be selling them too so he will not be able to charge much. If anything goes wrong with his lemon trees or if everyone suddenly decides that they do not want lemons, then he is in trouble. If he grew or made something else as well, he would not be so much at the mercy of the other traders. This is why countries that depend on one crop or product are trying to develop other ones (see page 13).

If you looked closely at the market-place, you would also see several one-person industries. Perhaps a tinsmith, a cobbler or someone repairing bicycles. Some of the world's largest companies grew from such small beginnings. Can you find an example? Let's have a look now at people working in industries and businesses.

You usually find a few people running small businesses in the market-place, like this Kenyan tinsmith. Some of the world's biggest companies began as a one-person business.

World trade is rather like a market-place where countries, rather than people, bargain over prices for raw materials like rubber, zinc, coffee and tea.

38

A small business – Morocco

The first step beyond being a one-person business, or a family business where everyone helps out, is when you decide there is enough trade to employ someone to work with you. Let's look at a small leather tannery in Morocco which has taken this step but is still run like a family business. The tannery is in a courtyard built near the old sea wall of Rabat. It lies in a street of tanneries. Doors open from the street onto a series of self-contained courtyards where both working and family life take place. The living accommodation is around the edge of the courtyard. This is for the family and for Abdul, Ibrahim and Mustapha, the young men employed by the tannery's **patron**, or owner. Work takes place in the middle.

All the city's tanneries are in this area because it is close to the slaughterhouses where the goatskins come from. After the skins have been scraped clean, the patron's two young sons trim off any awkwardly shaped or spoilt bits. They are paid for this job and usually do it after school. Mustapha, the tannery foreman, keeps a fatherly eye on them. The skins are then washed.

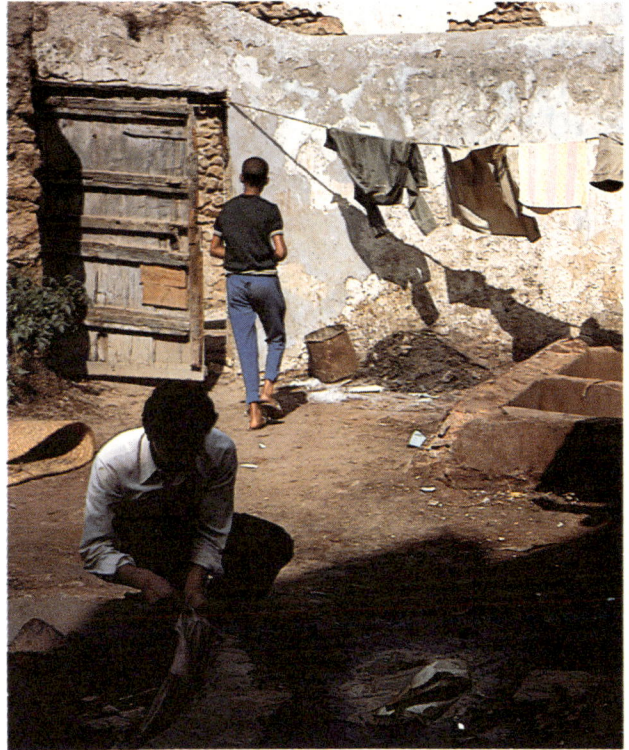

The tannery courtyard. Work takes place in the middle of the courtyard and everyone lives in rooms around the edge.

As soon as the goatskins have been fetched from the slaughterhouse they are scraped clean, trimmed and then thoroughly washed.

Meanwhile sacks of nuts, from which the dye for the leather is made, have been delivered to the tannery by country women on donkeys. Everyone carefully picks over the nuts to remove any stones or bits of wood or metal which might scratch the skins. Then they are ground between two stone wheels to make a pinkish-white powdery dye. This is mixed with water and poured into stone and clay wells set into the courtyard floor. This dye produces a natural light tan colour. A special root dyes the skins deep brown, **indigo** turns them dark blue and other dyes colour them red or green.

Abdul and Ibrahim start treading the skins into the dye vats or wells. It can take several hours because unless the skins soak up the dye thoroughly, the colour looks patchy and uneven. Afterwards, the skins are hung out to dry in the sun. Before long they are as stiff as a starched shirt. Then they are put over a wooden block and pummelled and beaten with a round wooden mallet to soften them. It makes the tannery sound like a school for drummers!

Abdul pulls a bucket of water up by rope from the courtyard well. He mixes the powdery dye with the water.

The dye is poured into stone and clay wells set in the courtyard floor. Abdul and Ibrahim tread the skins in the dye so that they soak it up thoroughly.

At this point the elderly patron, who spends much of the day sitting sleepily in the shade of a courtyard above, takes over. After a close inspection of the skins, he takes them off to Rabat's bustling **soukh** (market) to sell them to the craftsmen in the leather shops. The craftsmen make bags, shoes, slippers, purses, pouffes, wallets and cushions out of the leather. The patron runs the tannery well. He makes sure that they get skins and dyes of the best quality. He has taught Abdul, Ibrahim and Mustapha everything there is to know about the business.

In the evening Abdul, Ibrahim, Mustapha and the family sit outside in the still, cool air, smoking and chatting after their meal. Saturday is their day off but they usually spend it together, perhaps taking a boat down the river for a picnic, visiting friends and going to the Mosque. Do you know anyone who works in a small business? Is it run like this one? Do the people in the business live and work together?

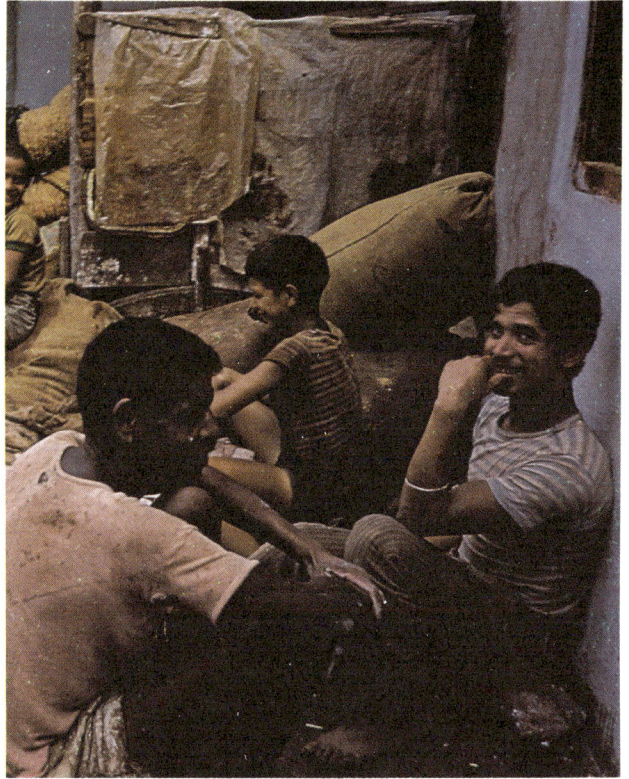

Everyone works, eats and lives together at the tannery. Abdul, Mustapha, Ibrahim, the patron and his sons and nephew are like brothers in a family business.

After the skins have been soaked in dye, they are dried in the sun and softened with wooden mallets. Can you see the living accommodation in this picture.

How is the business run?

Although Mustapha and the others at the tannery share their meals, accommodation, work and time off, the tannery is owned by the patron alone. Many businesses are like this, owned by an individual or a group of people. Others are owned by the State or the Government, such as Britain's British Rail or Australia's Post Office Services. Some are run as **collectives**. This means that everyone who works there owns the business together. There are examples of collectives in many countries. In China, since a new Government came to power in 1949, all factories and businesses are run this way.

A few of the old craftsmen, such as ivory and jade carvers, are still at work but they are now in cooperative groups and small factories. These are run by their local **commune** (a commune is a group of people who live and work together). The craftsmen are no longer working as individuals or in the old family businesses. The Chinese say a factory is like a machine. If one small screw is missing, the machine will not work properly so you cannot divide the jobs and say that one is more important or better than another.

A worker in a Chinese silk-painting factory. In China today even craftsmen work in commune factories, not on their own or in family businesses.

The factories in China are full of slogans encouraging everyone to work harder. Many have nurseries where the workers' young children are looked after all day..

42

Working life in Japan follows yet another pattern. The Japanese are very hard workers. Although they do not work in communes like the Chinese, they are very loyal to the company they work for and often stay with the same one throughout their working life. Members of the same company see themselves as part of one group. They often live in the same area, in flats which the company has helped them to buy. They spend their free time in the company's sports and social clubs. They go away together on holidays organised by the company. A Japanese worker is expected to be loyal and hardworking but in return he or she gets more than just a salary.

Try and find out how the various businesses and factories in your local area are organised. You may find several different types of working business. It may be a family business, like the bakery on this page, or a collective, or one owned by the State. Try and find out how often people change their jobs. How many people do you know who have been in the same job since they started work?

A family business in North London. Try and find out how the different businesses in your area are run and how many people have stayed in the job all their lives.

Japan has become a very successful industrial nation. The Japanese are often hard workers and usually stay with the same company all their working lives.

43

The holiday business

Many people work in **service industries**. These are businesses which meet a need or provide a service for people rather than making a product. Working in a shop is one example. One of the most rapidly growing service industries in the world today is the tourist industry.

Cheaper air travel has meant that more and more people are spending their holidays abroad. For some of the world's poorer countries, with sunny climates and beautiful scenery but poor soil for crops or few natural resources, tourism seemed a good way to earn money and improve life for their people. So hotels were built and holidays began, but tourism brought a few problems too.

Lamin Boya is a waiter at a seaside hotel in The Gambia. He enjoys his work and, during the tourist season, he earns more money than his father ever did. His father was a subsistence farmer with no chance of other employment. Building the hotels also provided work for Gambian construction workers, although many foreigners were employed too. Quite a lot of Lamin's friends now have jobs connected with tourism, driving taxis, working in restaurants or selling souvenirs.

Lamin, a waiter at a Gambian hotel. A tourist may spend more on a snack than Lamin earns all day.

One of the beaches in Barbados which attracts many tourists. A large number of the Caribbean population work in tourism.

You are probably still wondering what the drawbacks of tourism are? One is that tourists only come in certain seasons, so the hotels are empty and their employees out of work for months at a time. The food which the tourists want cannot always be produced locally, so it has to be bought and flown in from other countries. This uses up a lot of the money that tourism earns. The entertainments provided may be colourful and exciting, but they do not usually tell the tourist much about the everyday life of his hosts.

In fact, both the tourist and the host can get an unrealistic picture of each other. The tourists are there to escape from their everyday life. Sometimes they behave differently from the way they behave at home, occasionally in ways that might offend local customs. Some tourists only see their hosts in their working roles of waitress, shop assistant or hotel worker.

Have you ever had a holiday abroad? How much did you learn about the living patterns of the people there? Did you visit a family's home or meet any young people of your own age?

Basket sellers on a Barbados beach. In some countries traditional crafts have been revived by the demands from tourists for souvenirs.

Hotel entertainments often do not give the tourist a very realistic picture of the country they are visiting.

Time off from work

We have looked briefly at the job of looking after people who are enjoying an escape from work. Let's leave the subject of work now, and finish by looking at the way people relax in their time off. Perhaps it will tell us something about their working lives. Do you know what a 'busman's holiday' is? It is when somebody's holiday or time off is spent doing the same thing that they do at work. For example it may be a busdriver who spends his holiday motoring through the countryside, or a painter who decorates his own home.

This decorator is having a 'busman's holiday'. painting his own home.

One of the colourful processions at Trinidad's Mardi Gras festival, which lasts for two days and nights.

The Mardi Gras festival in Trinidad is certainly not a busman's holiday for the people who take part. The two days and nights of energetic dancing, colourful parades and crowded processions are a glorious escape from working life for everyone on the island. Yet the music and the costumes do tell us something about the Trinidadians' working lives, past and present. Some of the costumes remind us that many Trinidadians originally came from the Yoruba tribe of Nigeria. They were brought over by the old French and English plantation owners to work in the sugar cane fields.

The Mardi Gras festival is a combination of the French Mardi Gras, the Yoruba Festival of Images and Canboulay. Canboulay was originally an annual day's freedom at sugar harvest time. Plantation workers used to perform ceremonies using **cannes brulées** (burning sticks of sugar cane) as torches. Some of the Mardi Gras music is played to the rhythms of the old work songs sung by the plantation workers. The music used to keep them going in time with one another as they moved forward in lines, rhythmically and evenly cutting the sugar cane. So you can see that Mardi Gras tells us quite a lot about work and Trinidad.

Think about the festivals that are celebrated in your community and about the way people there spend their time off. Does it tell you anything about their working lives and living patterns? How do you spend your holidays and time away from school work? What do your parents do in their time off? Do they enjoy a complete break from work or do they have a 'busman's holiday'?

Some of the festival costumes remind us that many Trinidadians came originally from Nigeria to work in the sugar plantations. Some of the music reminds us of the work they did.

What you do and your family like to do when you are on holiday?

Index

Agricultural work 8, 16, 24, 26, 32

Bartering 9
Bolivia 24

Cash crops 8, 21
Cash economy 6, 8
Caste system 12
Change 17, 18, 21, 42
China 42
Collectives 42
Communes 42
Cooperatives 36
Craftsmen 9, 10, 11, 28, 41, 42
Crop growing 16, 21

Employment and self-employment 23, 25, 34, 35, 39

Family businesses 10, 39, 43
Festivals 32, 33, 47
Fishermen 16, 33

Gambia, The 44

Holidays 31, 32, 44, 46, 47
Housework 5, 14, 20
Hunters and gatherers 15

Kenya 11, 20

India 12, 22, 26
Iran 28

Japan 43

Machines 22
Malaysia 34
Markets 16, 38, 41
Mauritius 13
Migrant workers 23, 24, 25
Morocco 39

One-crop economies 12, 38

Plantation work
    cotton 24
    rubber 35
    sugar 13, 21, 47

Raw materials 37, 38
Religion 12, 33
Rubber 8, 34, 37

Seasonal work 24, 32, 45
Self-sufficiency 5, 7, 20
Service industries 44
Shift work 31
Small business 25, 38, 39
Smallholdings 20, 34
Specialised work 6, 9
Sri Lanka 7, 11
Subsistence economy 6, 7
    farming 8
Superstitions and taboos 18

Time off 30, 31, 46
Tourism 44
Trading 9, 16, 37, 38
Traditional work 10, 11, 16, 17, 18, 28
Trinidad 47

Women 5, 15, 16, 18, 20
Women's liberation movement 18
Working day, the 30
Working in the city 25, 26, 32, 33
World trade 37, 38